P-39 AIRACOBRA in action

by Ernie McDowell

illustrated by Don Greer

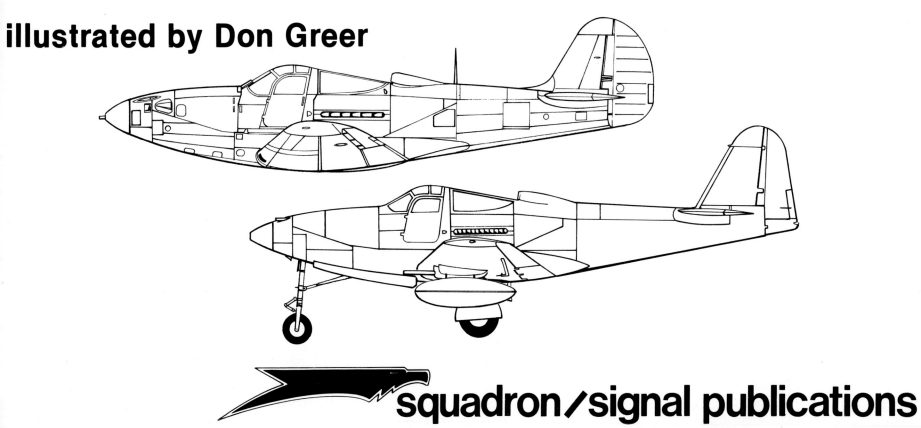

squadron/signal publications

(Cover) Over the deceptively beautiful Owen Stanley Range, Hawkeye II attracts the attention of a pair of Zeros. One of the original USAAF P-400s to move up to New Guinea, she still carries the pre-war style 'U.S. ARMY' under her wings.

ISBN 0-89747-102-4

If you have any photographs of the aircraft, armor, soldiers or ships of any nation, particularly wartime snapshots, why not share them with us and help make Squadron/Signal's books all the more interesting and complete in the future. Any photograph sent to us will be copied and the original returned. The donor will be fully credited for any photos used. Please send them to: Squadron/Signal Publications, Inc., 1115 Crowley Dr., Carrollton, TX 75011-5010.

DEDICATION: To the late Martin C. Haedtler, P-39 pilot and Dr. Richards H. Hoffman, Flight Surgeon.

A special acknowledgement of appreciation to Mr. Donald J. Norton and Mrs. Elaine H. Heise, both of Bell Aerospace/Textron, who proofread the text, to Mr. Royal Frey and the Staff of the USAF Museum. To Lt. Col. Terry Hemeyer, Capt. Peter R. Hefler and Mr. Dana Bell all of the USAF 1361st Photo Squadron, USAF Office of Information, to IPMS-USA, to IPMS-UK, IPMS-Finland, American Aviation Historical Society, FLAK and to Edward F. Furler, Jr., M. Sgt. David W. Menard USAF Ret., Al Makiel, Wyatt Exum and Ed Zdun.

Photo Credits

W. J. Balogh, Sr.	D. W. Luckabaugh
Bell Aerospace-Textron	E. Niccole
Dana Bell	D. W. Menard
Eugene Chudy	Al Makiel
Fred C. Dickey, Jr.	N. A. Nilsson
E. F. Furler, Jr.	Klaus Niska
M. C. Headtler	Juraj Rajninec
L. G. Hall	Felix Ramader
Chet Klish	Earl Reinert
Robert Kopitzke	Kenn C. Rust
George Letzter	Bill Thompson
M. Lavigne	Ralph Winkle
Malcom Long	

The first aircraft to use the recently reconquered airstrip on Makin Island in the Gilberts was this P-39Q-1, 42-19474, Little Rebel. Of interest is the spiral striping of the .50 cal MGs and the way that the bar of the national insignia is carried under the gunpod. 13 December 1943. (USAF)

Introduction

The Bell P-39 Airacobra, and its descendant the P-63 Kingcobra, represent perhaps the first application of "weapons system" thinking to aircraft design. The P-39, or the Bell Model 3 from which it derived, was only the second design to emerge from the new Bell Aircraft Corp. Robert J. Woods, Bell's chief designer, and his assistant Harland M. Poyer, saw a demonstration of a 37mm Oldsmobile cannon in 1935. Impressed by the power that this weapon represented, the pair decided to design an interceptor around the new cannon, the essence of a "weapons system".

The 37mm cannon was a formidable weapon but presented equally formidable problems to the designer, being much heavier than the normally-mounted MGs and generating much heavier recoil forces. Woods decided that the only practical position for this weapon was on the centerline. Since sychronizing such a weapon to fire through the propeller arc was considered too dangerous, Woods decided to mount the bulky cannon to fire through the propeller hub. This decision in turn led to the idea of mounting the engine amidships. The advantages of this position in improved handling was well known but the technical problems had always discouraged designers. Never one to fear to make a few waves, Woods reasoned that automobiles and ships had for years employed geared drive shafts, why not aircraft. And, having created a relatively vacant space in the forward section of the fuselage, Woods found room for a retracting nose wheel. The original model 3 design called for the cockpit behind the engine, the ideal location from the point of view of weight distribution, but the problem of visibility over the nose eventually forced a change to a more central position.

A modified mockup, designated Bell Model 4, was used as the basis for a submission to the USAAC on 18 May 1937. The Army Air Corps was impressed with the projected performance of Bell's fighter and ordered a single prototype to be designated the XP-39, on 7 October 1937.

The Bell Model 3 mockup, as of 24 May 1937. The mid-engine placement and cannon armament had already been established, only the cockpit placement was to change appreciably. (Bell)

(Above & Left) The Bell Model 4, alias XP-39, 38-326, was unveiled at Bell's Buffalo plant in Spring 1938. These more or less heavily retouched views show the arrangement of air scoops on either side of the fuselage. The supercharger intake was on the left side (left), the radiator/oil cooler inlet was on the right (above). (Bell)

Supercha

Prototype Airscoop

Radiator/
Oil C

XP-39

The Bell Model 4, re-christened the XP-39, serial number 38-326, was completed at Bell's Buffalo plant, crated and shipped to Wright Field, Ohio, assembled and first flown on 6 April 1938. It was an immediate success, demonstrating an excellent rate of climb and reaching 390mph at 20,000 ft. Powered by a supercharged Allison V-1710-17, rated at 1150hp, and equipped with none of the armament or armor that would inevitably be fitted to production models, this performance was, unfortunately, an illusion.

The XP-39 established the basic form and structure of the whole series. The oval, flush-riveted, all-metal fuselage was built in two main sections: the forward section that included the engine mounts and wing center section which was built around two longitudinal strength members and the cockpit deck plate, and the semi-monocoque aft section built up of bulkheads and stringers. The tail group was made up of all-metal fixed and fabric-covered control surfaces. Detachable panels made access to the armament, radio and engine exceptional. The wing outer panels joined at a point 22" out from the centerline. Three spars formed the wing structure. The Frise-type ailerons were fabric-covered. Split flaps formed the undersurface of the inboard trailing edge.

The cockpit canopy was glazed with six transparent panels, offering exceptional all-around visibility. Automobile type doors allowed access to the cockpit from either side, each door having a roll-down window.

The tricycle-type landing gear was composed of a single, self-castering, non-steering, rear-retracting nose wheel and large single inward-retracting main wheels. Retraction was electrical with manual back-up. Each wheelwell was completely covered by triple doors.

The mid-engine drove the propeller by means of a driveshaft running at crankcase speed under the pilot's seat. Early Airacobra pilots were fearful of the damage the drive shaft could do if it were to break loose or be damaged in combat. In practice it proved to be as safe or safer than the more conventional arrangement. The greater complexity of the mid-engine and the nose mounted reduction gearbox did cause problems in terms of reliability, the P-39 having a lower serviceability rate than its contemporaries. The exhaust system led to six ejector stubs on each side, changed to 12 per side on later models. The fuel system was composed of tanks totalling 60 gal. in the wing outer panels with a reserve tank of 20 gal. in the left wing.

The initial promise of the XP-39 was marred only by engine overheating problems. The cause was believed to be inadequate ventilation, resulting in the enlargement of both the left-side supercharger intake and the right-side radiator inlet and exhaust. When this didn't solve the problem, a re-examination proved that the overheating was caused by an easily-remedied structure in the oil system. With this revision, the XP-39 was endorsed for production with an order for 13 service test pre-production YP-39s (Bell Model 12) being made in April 1939. Meanwhile, the XP-39 was turned over to NACA at Langley Field for full scale wind tunnel tests.

As a result of the Langley tests, a number of alterations were suggested. The XP-39 was flown to Buffalo and revised, emerging in November 1939 as the XP-39B. (There was to have been an XP-39A, resulting from the installation of a V-1710-31 non-supercharged, high-altitude rated engine in one of the 13 YP-39s, but this was never done.) Most of the changes involved streamlining the airframe. The canopy was redesigned, resulting in a longer, lower shape. The oil cooler and radiator intakes were moved from the fuselage right side to the wing roots. The wing span was decreased from 35 ft. 10 in. to 34 ft. and length increased from 28 ft. 8 in. to 29 ft. 9 in. Perhaps the most noticeable change was the removal of the engine air intake from the left side of the fuselage to the dorsal centerline behind the cockpit. This was related to a more serious change, the replacement of the 1150hp V-1710-17 with a 1090hp non-supercharged V-1710-39 with a rated altitude of 13,300 ft. The reasoning behind this change reflected the curious state of USAAC thinking in the last months before the outbreak of WW II. While busy developing a pair of excellent strategic bombers (B-17 & B-24), USAAC planners felt that America's ocean barriers made her invulnerable to reprisal in kind. Therefore, the development of interceptor aircraft optimized for high-altitude performance was curtailed in favor of strike-fighters designed for low-altitude close-support. Thus in spite of a considerable reduction in drag due to the streamlining, the XP-39B suffered a considerable performance decrease. It now took 7½ minutes to reach 20,000 ft. instead of 5 and the maximum speed fell from 390mph at 20,000 ft. to 375mph at 15,000 ft. There was, however, an increase in low-altitude maneuverability and at low-altitude the performance loss was marginal. Therefore, in January 1940, the USAAC directed that 13 YP-39s be completed without superchargers.

(Above & Below) The XP-39B was the original prototype modified as a result of wind tunnel tests at NACA Langley. Note the difference in nose gear door design at various stages of the XP-39B's life. (Bell via W. Thompson & E. Chuddy)

P-39 Development

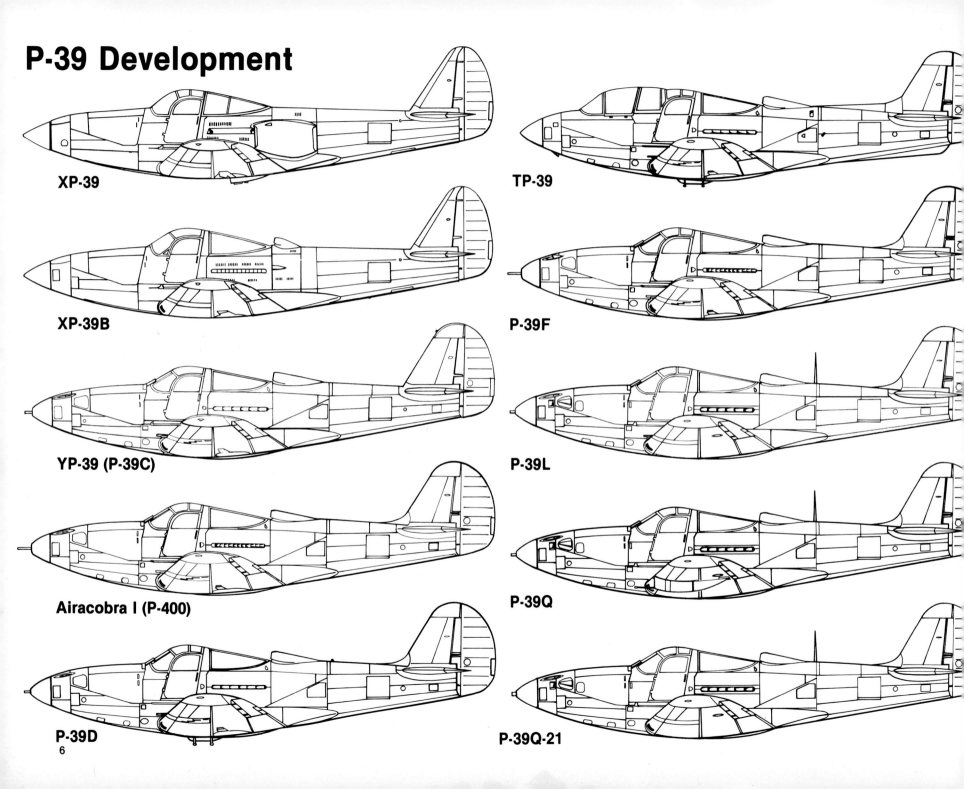

XP-39

XP-39B

YP-39 (P-39C)

Airacobra I (P-400)

P-39D

TP-39

P-39F

P-39L

P-39Q

P-39Q-21

YP-39 & P-39C (P-45)

The 13 Bell Model 12s, YP-39s, were ordered in April 1939 and revised in January 1940 to reflect the changes in the XP-39B. The first of the YP-39s, 40-27, flew on 13 September 1940 differing from the XP-39B primarily in having a larger vertical tail. The engine was changed again, the YPs being fitted with the Allison V-1710-37, also of 1090hp. More significantly, the service test aircraft carried complete armament, including the 37mm cannon with 15 rounds in the propeller hub plus a pair of .50 cal. MGs with 200 rpg and a pair of .30 cal. MGs with 500 rpg mounted in the cowling. In all, the additional equipment raised the all-up weight of the Airacobra to 7235 lb. (from the 6204 lb of the original XP-39). Performance now dropped to a maximum speed of 368mph at 15,000 ft. In spite of this continual degradation of performance, the USAAC claimed to be pleased with the Airacobra, ordering 80 production aircraft similar to the YP-39s.

The first production version of the Airacobra, the Bell Model 13, was ordered with a new designation, P-45. In spite of the fact that it was identical to the YP-39s, the political climate in 1940 wouldn't allow the Army Air Corps to acquire a new aircraft but would allow it to order an existing model. Therefore, the designation was changed again to P-39C, and production began in 1940. The first P-39C, 40-2971, flew in January 1941. Almost immediately the USAAC decided that the P-39C was inadequately protected for its role as a ground-support and ordered substantial additional equipment. So great were the changes that the new version was given a new designation. Only 20 Airacobras were completed to C standard, 40-2971—40-2990.

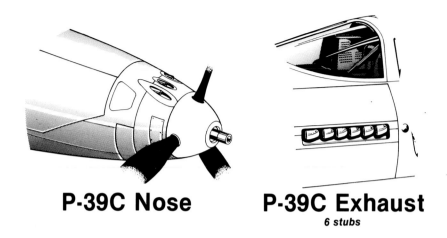

P-39C Nose

P-39C Exhaust
6 stubs

Only 20 of 80 P-39Cs ordered were completed to that standard. While all the Cs visible in this 31st Pursuit Group line-up at Selfridge Field, Michigan, have the production-style blunt spinner, only the second from the front appears to carry armament, early 1941. (USAF)

Four 31st PG Airacobras are seen lined up during the Fall 1941 Carolina Maneuvers. These yellow-nosed P-39Cs carry the white cross marking of the Blue Force. The yellow designators of earlier in the year have been replaced by black, low-visibility markings. The 40th PS insignia, a red devil on a white cloud, is carried on the door of No. 67. (Al Makiel)

Airacobra I (P-400)

When WW II broke out in Europe, the Allied Powers, Britain and France, were woefully short of modern aircraft with which to oppose the Axis. So great was the need for interceptors that when Bell submitted specifications to the British Direct Purchase Commission for a fighter with a top speed of 400mph, a ceiling of 36,000 ft. and a range of 1000 miles, an immediate order was placed for 675 Bell Model 14s, sight unseen on 13 April 1940. The performance which Bell claimed had indeed been achieved by the XP-39, but when the first Airacobra was delivered to RAF Duxford (actually a P-39C rearmed to British standard) it couldn't come close. Even when the first Model 14 arrived, powered by a 1150hp V-1710-E4, it still couldn't top 367mph. Besides the somewhat more powerful engine, the other difference in the Model 14, designated Airacobra I by the RAF, was in armament. The Model 14 carried a 20mm Hispano Mk1 cannon with 60 rounds in the propeller hub, two .303 Brownings in the cowling and two in each wing.

Tests with the AFDU at Duxford were extremely disappointing to the British. Expecting a nimble interceptor, they found that they had a troublesome close-support fighter. Besides the low top speed, other aspects of the Airacobra's performance were well below expectation, rate of climb, ceiling and take-off run being the most serious problems. Equally critical was the nasty habit of the compass to cease functioning after the cannon had been fired.

Mechanical problems were worked out during the period at Duxford, after which four Airacobra Is were issued to No.601 Sqdn at RAF Manston. A single mission was flown, a strafing run over France, on 9 October 1941. Two days later the four were back at Duxford. No further operations were flown and, in December, the Airacobra I was officially withdrawn from RAF service.

Of the 675 Model 14s ordered by the RAF, 212 were diverted to the Soviet Union (54 of that number being lost in transit), and 179 were taken over by the USAAF. Retaining their RAF serial numbers, over 100 of the Model 14s, designated P-400 in US service, were shipped to Australia in early 1942 to strengthen USAAF units there. Along with P-39Ds, the P-400 became one of the first USAAF aircraft to see action when the 8th Group took it into action over port Moresby, New Guinea, in April 1942. The RAF serials were in several series; AH728-738, AP266-283, BW100-183 and BX135-174.

All four Airacobra I's taken into operation by No.601 (County of London) Sqdn. are seen at Duxford. The winged sword on the RAF tail flush was that squadron's insignia. (E.J. Furler Jr.)

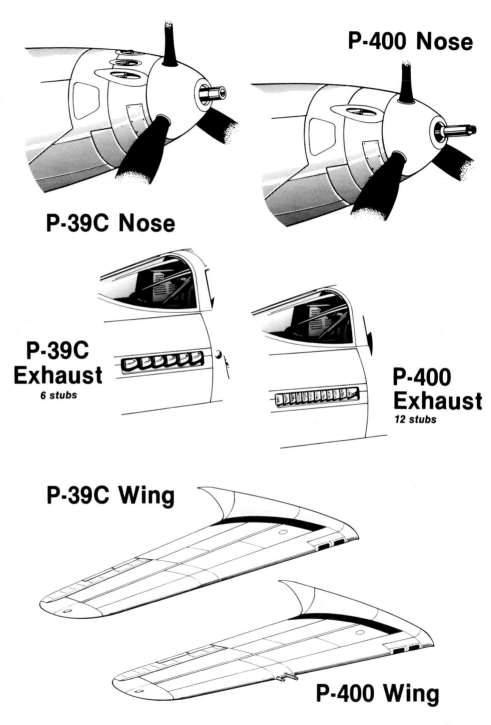

P-400 Nose

P-39C Nose

P-39C Exhaust
6 stubs

P-400 Exhaust
12 stubs

P-39C Wing

P-400 Wing

(Above) When the Airacobra I's, which the RAF refused, were taken on strength by the USAAF, they were redesignated P-400. This example is in absolutely standard RAF markings except for the USAAF roundels and the three digit number over the RAF fin flash, Laverton, Australia. (M. Long) (Below) A line-up of P-400s in Australia, probably at RAAF Laverton that was used as a trainng base. Gradually the RAF colors were replaced by OD and Neutral Gray. (M. Long)

Baptism by Fire

The 8th Fighter Group was sent to Australia, arriving in March to join the 35th which had reached there in February. The 8th was the first to see action as they were rushed to Port Moresby to relieve RAAF No. 75 Squadron. Forty-one Airacobras were dispatched from Townsville to Seven Mile Drome but only 26 arrived, the rest being lost enroute in crashes or forced landings. One of the pilots who on 28 April 1942 led a flight of eight 'Cobras, Col. Wyatt P. Exum, recalled the mission:

"I had arrived in Australia in April of '42 and in about two or three weeks was sent on up to New Guinea. I carried a flight of seven as just about everything we had there had been shot up or worn out. My mission mainly was to get there regardless of what happened to the pilots. I had a terrible time just trying to keep my flight in sight of each other, much

less in formation as these boys had at that time not been trained as fighter pilots. I had about five to six hours in a 'Cobra before leaving Townsville. The aircraft we were flying at that time were old. . .I think that they had 1,000 hours a piece flying time accumulated in the States. . .I believe that they had been at Langley Field. Unfortunately maintenance in this Group was absolutely terrible. The engines were running rough, records on the engines were inaccurate and very poorly kept, and, worst of all, the 36mm cannon had a very bad trajectory and if anybody ever hit anything with the 37mm I never heard of it. Everytime I tried to fire it—after one or two shots, sometimes maybe three—the gun jammed. I had an opportunity to fly a P-39 before going to Australia and that one was not loaded down with armor plate and leakproof tanks and I thought it handled beautifully. It was fast, maneuverable, and I was fairly well pleased when I got to Australia and found I was going to be in a P-39."

Col. Exum recalled another incident which though embarrassing did not prove to be tragic. "Bill Hornsby, my flight leader, and I were at the tail end of a formation, and when we saw Jap Zeros below us escorting a small number of bombers, we both peeled off and went after them. Before we got there, there seemed to be a dogfight going on. By the time we got to the Zeros we saw the dogfight consisted of Zeros playing around each other simulating a fight. Both Bill and I tried to get out of there and shot at anything that came by, Bill went by me and one of my bullets hit him and sent him into the drink. He returned to camp the next day, a little shook up but glad to be alive. Of course, I was even more glad to see him.

"As for dogfights with the Japs, there just were not any to my knowledge. If you had good position you could make a pass at the Japs and keep going. If the Nips had a good position on you, you half rolled and got the hell out of there. It was about as simple as that. The P-39 had a limited range so we did not fly much escort with the exception of one mission which we flew from Port Moresby to Wau. We escorted American C-47s carrying Australian special forces troops.

"I had one P-39 engine disintegrate with resulting complete loss of power during a scrap near the field at Port Moresby and had to leave the plane at less than 200 feet. At least, I can tell you it was an easy plane to get out of in an emergency. There is no doubt in my mind that if you stripped a P-39 and had a good engine (even the Allison in good shape) it could be a very fast airplane. A Tech Rep in Brisbane got permission to strip one and we heard that they could get 400 mph when normally the maximum cruise we were getting was 240-260 at 5 to 6,000 feet. The 'Cobra did not have a two stage blower, and as a result, although you could get from 260 to 300 mph on the deck, with every 1,000 feet of altitude the speed fell off, and the figure that sticks in my mind is that at 25,000 feet we got about 135 or 140 mph.

The very first combat mission of the Airacobra was flown by the 8th Pursuit Group's 35th and 36th Squadrons on April 30th, 1942. The official V Fighter Command Victory records devote a single line to that mission:
"Greene, George B. Jr. Major, 1 Zero, 15:07L, Salamaua 35th Sqdn." The official report submitted by Lt. Col. Boyd D. Wagner dated May 4th, 1942, tells a different story. "On Friday April 30th, 13 P-39Ds took off from Port Moresby on a ground strafing mission against Lae Airdrome, 180 miles North. Approach was made on Lae from 50 miles out to sea to avoid detection. When about 20 miles out 4 planes were sent ahead to engage the Japanese security patrol over Lae Drome. Top cover drew enemy security patrol off to the East of the drome and no resistance by air was encountered during the strafing. A line of 13 to 15 bombers were strafed on a sea approach in a three-three plane element. The planes in each element were disposed in echelon right. Our strafing planes were then attacked from above by several Zero fighters. Belly tanks were dropped immediately and throttles opened. Our formation began to pull away from the Zeros when the last four P-39s in the formation engaged in combat with three Zeros. In the meantime more Zeros appeared and it is estimated that there were 12-13 altogether. The P-39s were hopelessly outnumbered so the entire formation turned back and a terrific dogfight ensued. As a result of this low altitude dogfight four Zeros and three P-39s were shot down. All P-39s going down had been hit in the cooling system as a glycol spray could be seen streaming out behind while all Zeros shot down went burning. All three P-39 pilots were safe upon landing, either bailing out or crash landing on the beach."

"Macushla" and The Flaming Arrow, a pair of 35th PG P-400s served over New Guinea in early 1942, helping to break the momentum of the Japanese drive on Port Moresby. "Macushla" appears to have the beginning of a sharkmouth. The aircraft pictured below is The Flaming Arrow a few months later. The arrow is gone and she sports the finished sharkmouth. (M. Long)

Main Landing Gear

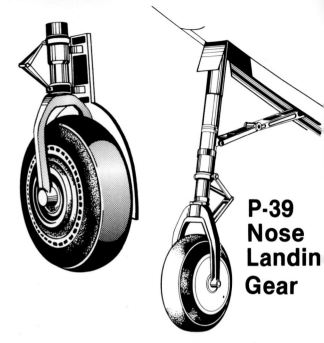

P-39 Nose Landing Gear

Another unit to fly the P-400 in combat was the 67th FS of the 347 FG which was based on New Guinea and Guadalcanal's Henderson Field in 1942. The Squadron's sharkmouth was carried on all aircraft. The Walt Disney designed Fighting Cock was an official marking. (Author)

An early P-39D, this HQ aircraft of the 31st PG was an umpire's aircraft during the Carolina Maneuvers in 1941. Note the segmented spinner and 31st PG insignia on the door. (Bell via E.H. Hartman & E. Furler)

P-39D

The remaining 60 Airacobras of the original 80 ordered as P-39Cs were completed to a revised design. The changes were primarily the installation of self-sealing fuel tanks and the strengthening and rearrangement of the armament. The 37mm cannon was now supplemented by a pair of .30 cal Browning MGs in each wing, with 1000rpg, the cowling now housing only a pair of .50 cals. Provision was also made for carrying stores on the centerline, either a 75 gal. drop tank or a 500 lb. bomb. Under the designation P-39D, Bell Model 15, a further contract for 343 was awarded. USAAF serials were 40-2991—3050 for the original 60, and 41-6772—7115 for the second contract.

Further Ds were produced primarily for Lend-Lease to Russia:

P-39D-1 (Bell Model 14 A)—This was a P-400, retaining the 20mm cannon but having .30 cal MGs in place of the .303s. A small dorsal fillet gave the tail a new shape, standard on all later P-39s and retrofitted to most earlier Ds. Serials were 41-28257—28406, 41-38220—38404 and 41-38563.

P-39D-2—Introduced the 1325hp V-1710-63 and re-introduced the 37mm cannon. Otherwise, it was identical to the P-39D-1. Serials: 41-38405—38562.

P-39-D-3 & —P-39-D-4—These were earlier Ds modified for ground attack duties, with oil cooler and radiator armor and two cameras mounted in the rear fuselage. They retained the V-1710-35 engine. They all saw action in Italy.

The P-39D, along with the P-400, was the first to see combat. Experience soon pointed out a great many weak points in the design, beyond the overall problem of poor altitude performance. Among the most serious was the lack of gun heaters which made the guns useless over 25,000 ft., the lack of hydraulic chargers which made the guns difficult to charge in the air and the forward gear box which had a tendency to throw oil.

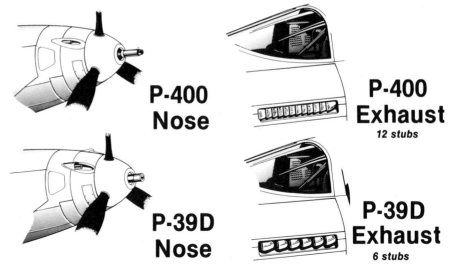

P-400 Nose

P-400 Exhaust
12 stubs

P-39D Nose

P-39D Exhaust
6 stubs

A P-39D-1 has virtually every panel and port open for inspection and work. The engine was very easy to work on, but the armament accessing was considered poor. Some Ds had the radio mast, but most did not. The .50 cal cowl guns were given a noticeable air scoop around the breech. (Bell)

Belly Rack

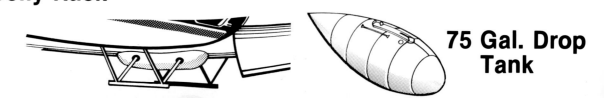

75 Gal. Drop Tank

Inside of Door

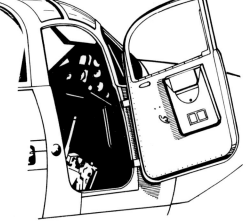

The cockpit of the P-39D was considered spacious and well-laid out in general, but the placement of the gun charging handles at the bottom of the control panel made them hard to use. Each model change brought some alteration of the control panel layout.

Swamp Rat, a C-47 of the 6th Troop Carrier Squadron is being escorted to a drop zone near Wau, New Guinea, by a quartet of P-39Ds of the 35th FG, April 1943. (USAF)

The first Aircobras to arrive in Hawaii were the P-39Ds of the 47th PS of the 15th PG, seen here at Wheeler Field. Note that '85' has a radio mast while the others don't. (Al Makiel)

This P-39D-1 of the 35th FG carries a white spinner, nose numeral (71), code letter (B) and fin tip. Few Airacobras carried the complete serial number. (Author)

Tail Fillet

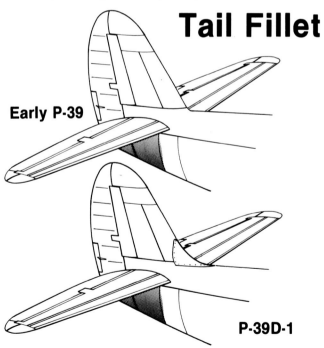

Early P-39

P-39D-1

Bell test airframe No. 14 was one of the prototypes for the Model 15 which, with self-sealing tanks and armor, became the P-39D. The airframe, registered NX-BA14, continued on in the role of testbed until its disposal. (Bell via E. Chuddy)

17

Middle Production Airacobras (P-39F - P-39N)

The next production model was the P-39F (Bell Model 15B). (There was an XP-39E. Three airframes used to test various parts of the P-63 design, described later.) As can be ascertained from the model number, it was a close relative of the preceding P-39D. The propeller was changed from the original Curtiss-Electric to an Aeroproducts constant speed model, but this made little difference in the appearance. As with the P-400, the P-39F had 12 exhaust stubs per side. Serials were 41-7116—7344. Some field-modified Fs became P-39F-2s with the addition of cameras in the rear fuselage.

At this stage of the war, the "dash" system of sub-dividing model changes wasn't in effect, and relatively minor changes brought letter changes in the series:

P-39G (Bell Model 26)—Intended to be identical to the P-39D-2 except for the new propeller. 1800 were ordered but none ever being completed as Gs.

P-39H & P-39I—Designations never assigned.

P-39J—These were the last 25 P-39Fs with a new engine, the V-1710-59 with automatic boost control. Externally identical. Serials: 41-7043—7056 and 41-7059—7079.

P-39K—First of the redesignated Gs, the 210 produced were basically identical to the P-39D-2 except for the propeller. They retained the D-2's more powerful -63 engine. Sometimes called P-39K-1. Serials: 42-4244—4453.

P-39L—These differed from the K in reverting to the Curtiss propeller. 250 were produced. Gross weight was now up to 9100 lbs., however the more powerful engine gave better low-altitude performance. A new nose wheel of somewhat different design offered less drag on take-off. Provision was made for rocket rails to be fitted. Serials: 42-4454—4703.

P-39M—The next 240 of the G order were given a new engine, the 1200hp V-1710-67 which gave poorer low-altitude performance but was 10mph faster at 15,000 ft., 370mph. This fell off rapidly at higher altitudes. The Aeroproducts propeller was again used. Serials: 42-4704—4943.

P-39M-1—This sub-variant was fitted with the -83 engine of similar characteristics as the -67. The Curtiss-Electric propeller was used. Serials were from the P-39M block.

P-39N—2095 of all three sub-variants were produced. The first 166 had normal fuel capacity, but later examples had four wing cells removed, lowering internal capacity to 87 gal. 75 gal. or 175 gal. belly tanks were standard. This kept weight down but often restricted range. Therefore kits were made available that allowed the four cells to be field-fitted. The V-1710-85 replaced the -67 and -83, but had the same power and characteristics. The Aeroproducts propeller was enlarged to 11 ft. 7 in. diameter, an increase of 6 in. Serials: 42-4944—5043 and 42-8727—9126. The N-1 sub-variant differed only in an alteration in the center of gravity. Serials: 42-9126—9726, 42-18246—18545.

P-39N-5—The main differences between this and the earlier versions of P-39N were the removal of 38 lbs. of armor, reducing the total to 193.4 lb., the replacement of the SCR-535A radio and the addition of a small armor plate to protect the pilot's head. Serials: 42-18546—19240.

P-390 & P-39P—designations never assigned.

(Above) Among the first Airacobras sent to Europe in USAAF colors was this example seen at Bassingbourne, England, enroute to North Africa for the 'Torch' landings. This is probably a P-39F, its RAF serial number lies outside the Aircobra I series. (USAF) (Below) A number of the P-39Fs en route to the 'Torch' landings landed in Portugal due to mechanical failures or navigational error. They were interned by the Portugese who put them to use. This example is seen at No. 2 Ota in 1944. (E. Furler)

(Below Left) Another theater in which P-39Fs saw action was Alaska. This F of the 57th FS, 54th FG, is having its engine worked on, July 1942. (USAF)

Air-A-Cutie, a P-39F of 36th FS, 8th FG, flew over New Guinea in 1943. The white nose band was the SWPA marking. The spinner, 'Q' and tail tip are also in white. (Author)

(Above) A line-up of P-39Js, which differed from the preceding F only in engine fit, sits at a stateside training base. (Author) (Below) The P-39K reverted to six exhaust stubs. Battlin' Annie, also known as Pat, takes off from a New Guinea airfield, 1943. (Major N. Flack)

(Above) Three P-39Ls wait on a quay alongside an escort carrier at a North African port. They will be loaded aboard and returned to the US for repair. All three are in RAF camouflage and have roundels with yellow surround. (D.W. Lucabaugh)

A mid-production Airacobra, probably a P-39L, sports figure of an angelic, angry Donald Duck on its nose. Two extra gas vents at the nose began to appear at this time. Lt. William F. McDonough, on the right, got two victories in '23' over Wau, New Guinea, 1943. (USAF)

(Above) This P-39N of the 18th FG waits at Henderson Field, Guadalcanal, June 1943. (USAF Museum) (Left) Pat, a P-39N of the North African Coastal Command flew with the Free French Air Force from Algeria. While all Airacobras from the D on were equipped to carry a 500 lb. bomb, few ever did. (USAF)

Spare Parts was created by the mechanics of the Skyraider Squadron in the Central Pacific from hulks and scrap. Painted black, with a question mark in the place of a serial number, she was used as a night fighter. (USAF)

Four views of 'door art' on P-39s of the 110th TRS at Gusap, New Guinea, Border Buckaroo II, also known as "Black Fury", was flown by Lt. DeVore. Superstitious, belonged to Lt. Kennon. Bucko and Mike was the mount of Capt. Lonigan. Posing on the wing is crew chief S/Sgt. Derenzo. "Billy the Kid" was flown by Lt. O'Connor. (Capt P. Giguere via Kenn Rust)

P-39Q

The final main production variant of the Airacobra was the P-39Q, 4905 of which were built before production ended. The first sub-type, the Q-1, serials 42-19446—19595, retained the 87 gal. fuel capacity but returned to the original 231.41 lb. of armor plate. The most significant difference was the deletion of the four .30 cal. wing guns in favor of a pair of .50 cal. in pods under the wing. This move was applauded by most pilots who generally felt that the .30 cal. was too light to be effective and that it wasn't worth the fuel to carry 4000 rds. The irony is that very few American pilots were ever to fly the Q, as nearly all were exported, primarily to Russia. The last USAAF units to fly the Airacobra, the 332nd FG in Italy, received 75 Qs in February 1944. After only two months, the Airacobras were replaced by P-47s, retiring the type from US service.

Other variants of the P-39Q included:

P-39Q-5—This variant reverted to the lighter armor fit of the N-5, as well as full wing fuel capacity.

P-39Q-10—Internal fuel capacity rose to 120 gal. and armor weight to 227.1 lb. Serials: 42-20546—21250.

P-39Q-15—Differed from the -10 in minor equipment changes. Serials‘ 44-2001—3000.

P-39Q-20—The underwing MG pods were deleted from this and all subsequent variants. Serials: 44-3001—3940, not all numbers from this series.

P-39Q-25—The export version of the -21, completely identical. Serials: 44-32167—32666 and 44-70905-71104.

P-39Q-30—The last Airacobra variant, which reverted to the three-bladed propeller. Serials: 44-71105—71504.

Total Airacobra production reached 9584 before the line was shut down in September 1944.

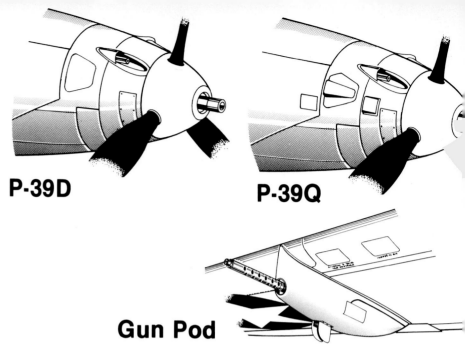

P-39D   **P-39Q**

Gun Pod

Tarawa Boom De-Ay **is a P-39Q-1 of the 318th FG based on Oahu, Hawaii.** My Gal Sal IV **is in the background. Qs appear to carry the radio mast as a standard fitting. (USAF)**

P-39Q

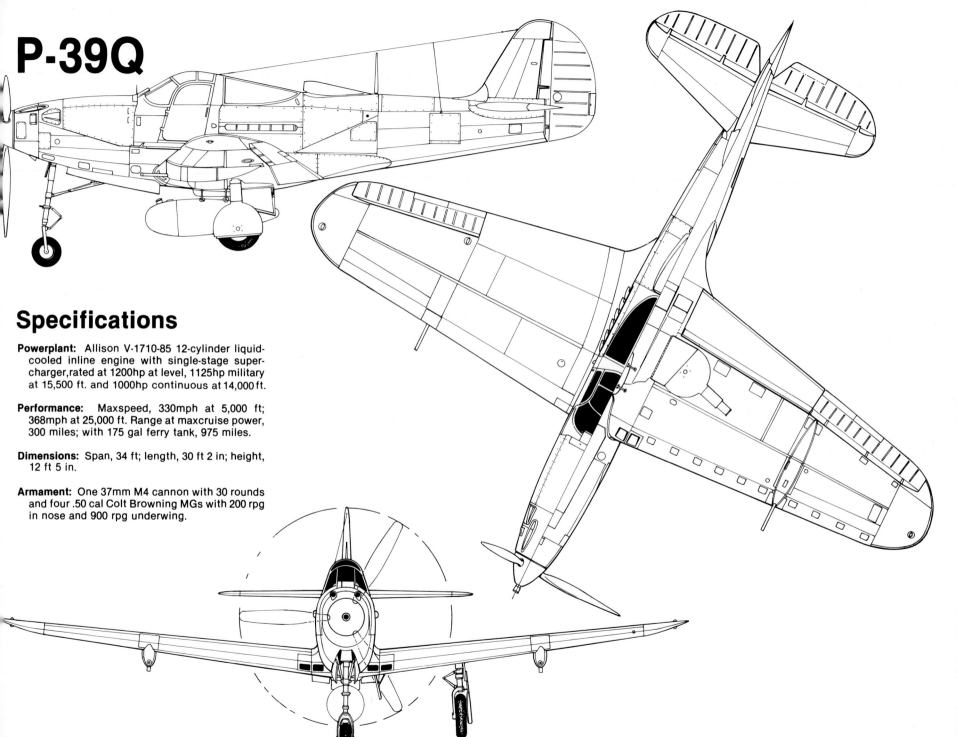

Specifications

Powerplant: Allison V-1710-85 12-cylinder liquid-cooled inline engine with single-stage supercharger, rated at 1200hp at level, 1125hp military at 15,500 ft. and 1000hp continuous at 14,000 ft.

Performance: Maxspeed, 330mph at 5,000 ft; 368mph at 25,000 ft. Range at maxcruise power, 300 miles; with 175 gal ferry tank, 975 miles.

Dimensions: Span, 34 ft; length, 30 ft 2 in; height, 12 ft 5 in.

Armament: One 37mm M4 cannon with 30 rounds and four .50 cal Colt Browning MGs with 200 rpg in nose and 900 rpg underwing.

Maxine, a P-39Q-20 retains the underwing pods though most late Qs did not. The rear-view mirror on the canopy was probably a field modification. (Fred Dickey)

Sgt. Ralph Winkle, crew chief for Snooks, poses in front of his ward, a P-39Q-5, 42-20351 seen on 5 March 1944. Snooks was the mount of 1st Lt. William Shomo of the 71st TRS, 82nd TRG, whose later exploits in a P-51 won him the Medal of Honor. (Ralph Winkle)

This P-39Q-5 shows off regulation SWPA markings, a white nose band, wing leading edge and tail. Note the relatively rare bomb on the centerline. (Author)

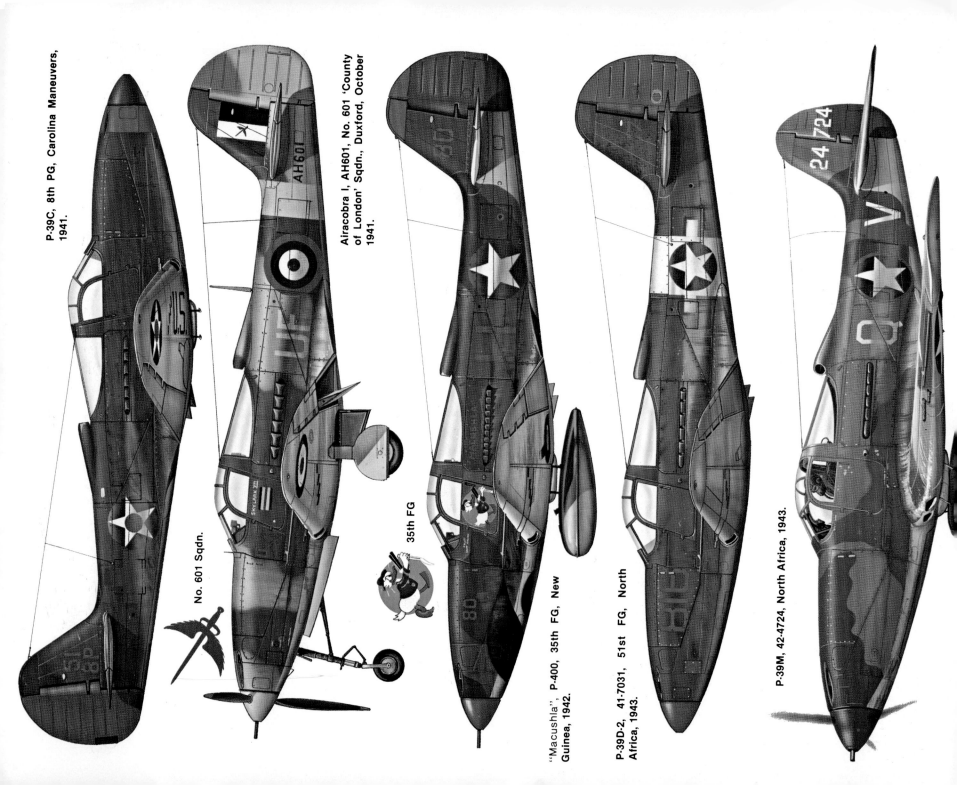

P-39C, 8th PG, Carolina Maneuvers, 1941.

Airacobra I, AH601, No. 601 'County of London' Sqdn, Duxford, October 1941.

No. 601 Sqdn.

35th FG

"Macushla", P-400, 35th FG, New Guinea, 1942.

P-39D-2, 41-7031, 51st FG, North Africa, 1943.

P-39M, 42-4724, North Africa, 1943.

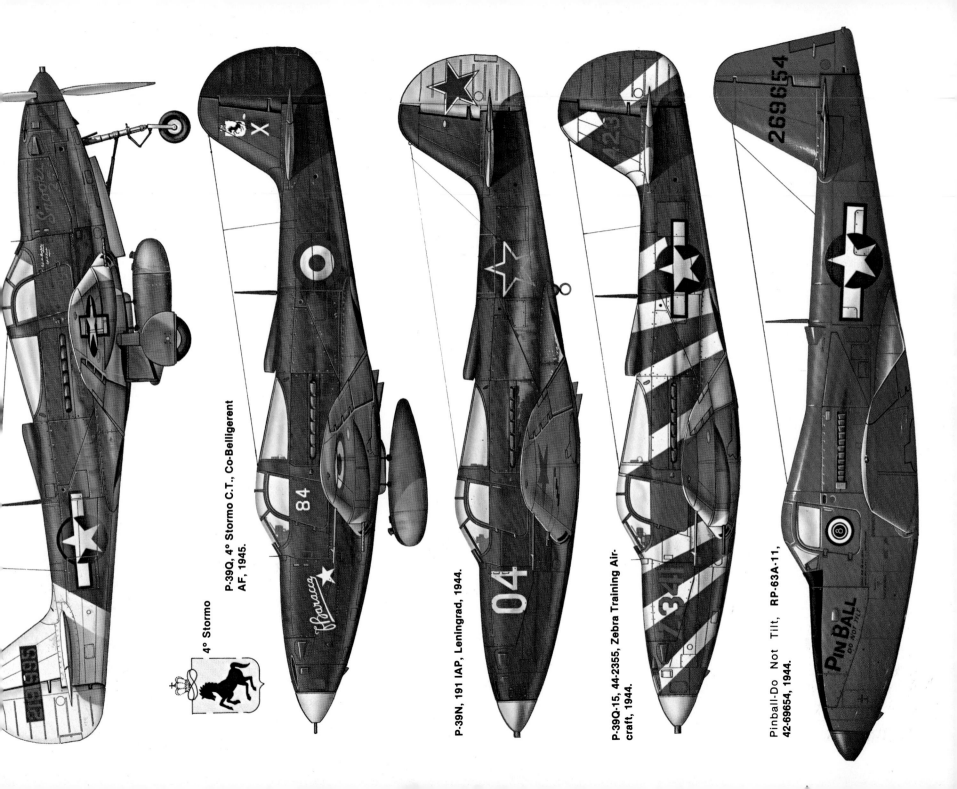

P-39Q, 4° Stormo C.T., Co-Belligerent AF, 1945.

4° Stormo

84

Sbaracca

P-39N, 191 IAP, Leningrad, 1944.

04

P-39Q-15, 44-2355, Zebra Training Aircraft, 1944.

34

Pinball-Do Not Tilt, RP-63A-11, 42-69654, 1944.

269654

PINBALL
DO NOT TILT

Flying with GC II/6 "Travail" based in Southern, France during the winter of 1944-45, this P-39Q-20 carries that Group's insignia, a white stork in a blue diamond. (Al Makiel)

This P-39Q-20 was used to raise funds for the 'Smokes for Soldiers' program run by the Buffalo Evening News. Funds carried on this bird totalled $4144.04 (Bell via E. Hartman & E. Furler)

Parked on the ramp at Salento Airfield, these P-39Qs of the 4° Stormo CT of the Co-Belligerent Air Force replaced Macchi C.202s on strength in that unit. They flew primarily over the Balkans.

Capt. P. S. Tshepinog, Hero of the Soviet Union, poses in front of his Airacobra, 24 victory stars painted above the exhaust. He flew for the 1st Ukrainian Front, April 1945. (IPMS Finland-Klaus Niska)

(Above Left) Two P-39Q-25s on the ramp at Buffalo. Note the lack of underwing gunpods. They were paid for by public subscription. They carry the inscription 'East Aurora, NY Public Schools'. The insignia is a red devil riding a bullet. (Bell via Al Makiel)

These P-39s were captured by the Finns and are seen in storage in 1947. One of these still survives and is being restored. (IPMS Finland-Klaus Niska)

As a B-17 of the 97th BG comes in for a landing at Poltava, two late P-39Qs of a Guards unit sit on the grass next to the runway. These Airacobras have neither wing nor underwing MGs. (Bob Jones)

A number of P-39s were converted into two-place trainers by adding a canopy in front of the original. The tail fillet was enlarged and an additional shallow fin was fitted under the rear fuselage. V-99 was formerly a P-39Q-5, now designated TP-39. (W. Thompson, Balogh via Menard and Al Makiel)

P-63 Kingcobra

In spite of the "mixed reviews" that the P-39 received, a derivative, the P-63 Kingcobra, was the only one of nine new fighter designs tested by the USAAF in 1942-3 to be produced in quantity. (The USAAF was obviously aware that the bulk of the Airacobra's problems was due to it being underpowered and lacking a supercharger, not to design deficiency.) Contrary to appearances, the P-63 was a totally new aircraft. Despite the similarity of arrangement with the Airacobra, no parts of the two aircraft were interchangeable. Perhaps most extraordinary was the fact that, although 3303 Kingcobras were produced, it never flew combat in USAAF markings.

Bell was also well aware of the reasons why the Airacobra hadn't lived up to expectations. In February 1941, the company proposed the Model 23 mating the basic P-39 to an uprated engine and a laminar flow wing. Three prototypes were ordered in April, to be designated XP-39E. Each of the three tested different wing and tail designs. The wing root intakes were enlarged. Originally intended to be powered by the Continental V-1430-1, they reverted to the 1350hp V-1710-47. Top speed was 393mph at 24,000 ft., but the XP-39Es were considered to be inferior to the basic Airacobra in all other respects. Serials were 41-19501—19502 and 42-7164.

So promising was the projected performance of the new design that, on 27 June 1941, before the first flight of the XP-39E, the USAAF ordered two prototypes of an enlarged fighter powered by the same V-1710-47, to be designated XP-63.

The Kingcobra was larger in all dimensions than the Airacobra. The wings were completely redesigned, of a NACA laminar flow design that reduced drag by a significant factor and increased span by 4 ft. 4 in. A laminar flow wing achieves its reduction in drag by delaying the onset of boundary-layer turbulence. This is achieved by a redesigned wing cross-section, but any benefit can be cancelled out by turbulence caused by minute ripples in the wing surface. NACA Langley was fearful that mass-production techniques wouldn't produce wings of sufficient smoothness, that test results obtained with hand-built prototypes couldn't be repeated by assembly line products. Bell rose to the challenge, using a series of mahogany gages at all stages of wing production. NACA's fears proved to be groundless.

The XP-63 was powered by the Allison V-1710-47 of 1325hp, but finally with a second, hydraulic turbocharger supplementing the normal single-stage, effectively adding 10,000 ft. to the service ceiling. One of the complaints against the Airacobra, that the armament wasn't easily accessible, was overcome in the P-63. Larger cowling panels allowed all guns to be replaced, and armed in 18 minutes, compared to the several hours that job would take with a P-39. The Kingcobra's armament was identical to the P-39Q's, a single 37mm cannon and two .50 cal in the nose and two more .50 cal in under wing gunpods. A four-bladed propeller was standard.

The XP-63, 42-15911, flew on 7 December 1942, the significance of the date being lost on no-one. The prototype weighed in at 7486 lb. (the USAAF specs called for a 7500 lb. gross weight). On 28 January 1943, the prototype was written off when the landing gear wouldn't extend due to a broken universal. The pilot, Jack Woolams circled the airport for several hours to burn up fuel, during which time the sun had set. Attempting the belly-landing in the deepening dusk, Woolams mistook runway side lights for end lights and put the XP-63 down in field of small trees. It was a testimony to the Bell design that Woolams walked away from the wreck. The second prototype, 42-15912, didn't last too much longer. Having first flown on 4 March, it crashed on 25 May 1943 when the engine threw a rod at altitude.

The original contract had called for only two prototypes, but after the loss of No. 2, the USAAF requested that the static test airframe, 42-78015, be completed in flying condition, with as much standard production equipment as possible. All up weight rose to 7660 lbs, but performance was still excellent. Designated XP-63A, this prototype differed mainly in being fitted with the V-1710-93 of similar characteristics as the -47. External differences included the fitting of wing racks, a redesigned dorsal air scoop and 12 rather than 6 exhaust stubs per side.

Bell's Wheatfield assembly lines produced P-39s and P-63s alongside each other. Two lines of P-39Q-30s are to the right, then come three lines of P-63As, another two of P-39Qs and one of P-63A-8s. (Bell)

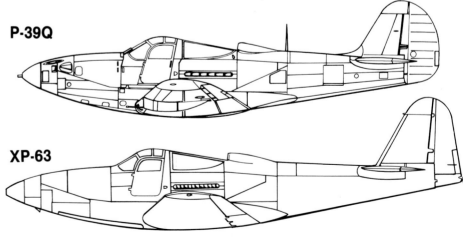

P-39Q

XP-63

The three XP-39Es were the testbeds for the Kingcobra series, trying out various configurations of wing and tail. (Right) No. 1 looked very similar to the P-63 with laminar-flow wing and vertical tail much like the Kingcobra's. The tail plane had squared-off tips. (Below) No. 2 had a squared-off fin and rudder and large fillet. (Below Right) No. 3 had all flight surfaces clipped. (William Thompson)

Two views of the first XP-63, 42-19511. This aircraft was lost in a belly-landing on 28 January 1943 when the landing gear failed to extend. Despite the loss of both initial prototypes, the USAAF was pleased with the Kingcobra's performance. (William Thompson)

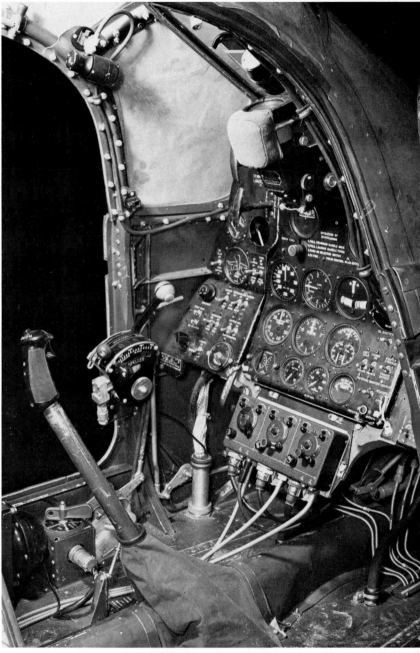

The main instrument panel of the XP-63. Again, as with the Airacobra, each change of equipment brought substantial changes in the layout of the panel. (Bell)

Production Kingcobras
(P-63A & P-63C)

P-63A-1—(Bell Model 33)-Virtually identical with the XP-39A. It was fitted with 87.7 lb. of pilot armor and had an internal fuel capacity of 100 gal. Serials : 42-68861—68910.

P-63A-5—This model introduced the dorsal radio mast which was standard on all later models. Pilot armor increased to 178.8 lb. A 75 gal. or 175 gal. fuel tank, or a 500 lb. bomb could be carried on the centerline. Top speed was 405mph. Serials: 42-68911—68930.

P-63A-6—Wing racks were fitted that could carry either a 75 gal tank or a 500 lb. bomb under each wing. Serials: 42-68931—69060.

P-63A-7—An increase in wing loading limited this variant to a 64 gal. tank under each wing. Serials: 42-69061—69210.

P-63A-8—188.8 lbs. of armor increased wing loading again. An improved version of the Aeroproducts propeller, the A6425-D3, increased top speed to 417mph. Serials: 42-6921—69410.

P-63A-9—Armor weight rose again to 198.9 lb. Ammo for the nose cannon rose from 30 to 58 rounds. Serials: 42-69411—69860. Five were converted to RPs.

P-63A-10—These were fitted with rocket rails. Armor increased again to 236.3 lbs. Serials 42-69861—69879 and 42-69975—70685.

P-63B—An intended version to be powered by the Rolls Royce Merlin V-1650-5 of 1400hp. Never built.

P-63C-1—The engine was changed again to the V-1710-117 which had the same normal rating but could be pushed to 1500hp in an emergency. Internal fuel capacity rose to 107 gal. Armor dropped to 201.3 lbs. The most noticeable change was the addition of a ventral fin under the aft fuselage. Serials: 42-70686—70860 and 43-10893—10932.

P-63C-5—Virtually identical except for the provision of centerline and wing racks. The last major production variant of the series. Serials 43-11133—11717.

P-63D—A single example externally similar to the A except that it had a sliding bubble canopy, the canopy doors being deleted. The engine was the V-1710-109 rated at 1425hp, pushing top speed to 436mph. The wing span was increased by 10 in. The serial was 43-11718.

P-63E (Bell Model 41)—This was the "production" version of the P-63D. It reverted to the standard canopy but retained the uprated engine and increased wing span. It had the ventral fin of the C model. 13 were produced. Serials: 43-11720—11721 and 43-11725—11735.

P-63F—Similar to the E except that a much taller fin and rudder were fitted. Serial 43-11719.

P-63 Development

P-63A-5

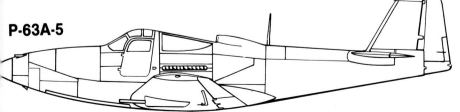

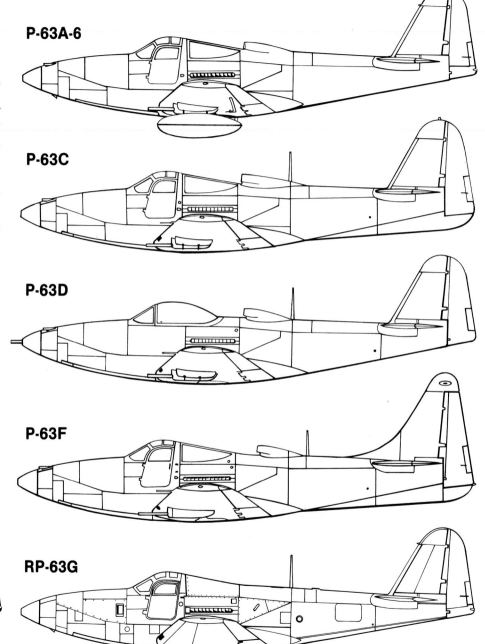

P-63A-6

P-63C

P-63D

P-63F

RP-63G

A pair of views of a pair of P-63A-9s seen in the sky over upstate New York. 450 of this dash-type were built, differing in the amount of ammo carried for the nose cannon and in the weight of armor, but externally identical to the preceding mark. (Bell)

P-63A

Specifications

Powerplant: Allison V-1710-93 12-cylinder liquid-cooled inline engine with single-stage super-charger, and auxilliary hydraulic turbo-charger,rated at 1325hp at sea level, 1150hp at 22,400.

Performance: Max speed, 361mph at 5,000 ft; 410mph at 25,000 ft. Range at max cruise power, 450 miles; with 175 gal ferry tank, 2575 miles. Service Ceiling, 43,000 ft.

Dimensions: Span, 38 ft, 4 in.; length, 32 ft 8 in; height, 12 ft. 7 in.

Armament: One 37mm M4 cannon with 58 rounds and four .50 cal Colt Browning MGs with 200 rpg in nose and 900 rpg underwing.

(Above & Right) The initial P-63A-6, 68931, after it tested the wing racks (not yet fitted in the above view) which were introduced on that mark, was used to test a ski landing gear. It passed all the tests on frozen Lake Ouimet, but was never placed in production. (USAF Museum)

This P-63A-9 was used as a testbed by Aeroproducts, whose insignia is carried on the nose. (E. Chuddy)

Edythe Louise was a P-63A-10, seen here without the underwing gun pods, with two 75 gal. drop tanks. This mark could be fitted with rocket rails. (USAF Museum)

Line after line of P-63A-10 wait outside the Bell factory to begin the long delivery flight to Russia. They have USAAF serials along with Russian stars. (Bell)

Bell's chief test pilot, Jay Demming, tries out this P-63A-9. The white circle around the red star was a delivery marking not often used on Kingcobras. (Bell via Hartman & Furler)

Over 100 P-63C-5s are visible in this view, giving some idea of the immensity of US aid to the Soviets in WWII. These have apparently been trapped by bad weather at Nome AB enroute to Siberia, Spring 1945. (USAF)

Sporting French markings, but seen over the flat farmland of upstate New York, this P-63C-5 shows the prominent ventral fin which characterized the C. (Bell)

P-63A Tail

P-63C Tail

(Above & Right) The sole P-63D was 43-11718. It was identical to an A except for engine, wingspan and canopy. At 437mph, the D had the performance that had long eluded the 'Cobras' but since this performance was no better than the P-51D's, which was already in production, no serious thought was given to mass-production. (Wm. Thompson & USAF Museum)

(Below Right) A close up of the sliding canopy of the P-63D. (National Archives via Dana Bell)

A single P-63A-9 was converted by the RAF to a bubble canopy, 42-69423, FZ440. Despite the sliding canopy, the lower halves of the cockpit doors were retained. (Bell)

The last production mark of the Kingcobra was the P-63E, Bell Model 41. At 439mph it was the fastest of the 'Cobras'. It returned to the standard canopy and ventral fin extension of the C but retained the engine and increased wing span of the D. (William Thompson)

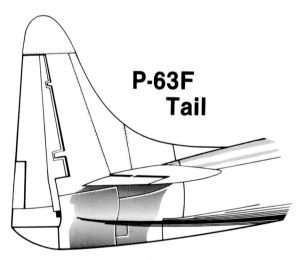

P-63F
Tail

Sitting in a surplus dump, awaiting disposal, this P-63E represents the fate of all USAAF Kingcobras, whose active service didn't outlast the war. (William Thompson)

The saga of the P-63F, the last of the Kingcobras. (clockwise from above) The sole prototype, 43-11719, had an extended vertical tail for better control, as well as the ventral extension. Postwar, it was sold several times, acquiring the civil designation N1719, retaining the last four digits of its USAAF serial. It finish 10th at the Thompson Trophy Races in 1946, now with an 'X' for experimental added to its registration. In 1959 it was on display at Mt. Hawley, IL, in very attractive blue and white markings with yet another serial. Its most recent appearance was at the 1976 Mojave Races where it finished 4th. (Thompson, Brown via Menard and Stevens)

"Flying Pinballs"

232 Kingcobras were built as RP-63s, which were put to possibly the most unusual use of any production aircraft—flying targets. They were flown against B-17s and other bombers in what had to be the most realistic gunnery training ever, because the gunners were able to fire directly at the Kingcobras and hits could be seen. A light in the propeller hub would light when a hit was scored giving rise to the "pinball" nickname. How was it done without recruiting suicidal pilots? The answer lay in up to a ton of external armor plate and a specially developed "frangible" bullet of lead and graphite compound that would shatter on impact. The first RPs were five P-63A-9s taken off the production line and specially modified, redesignated RP-63A-11. All internal armor was removed as was all armament and the entire fuselage was reskinned with heavy sheet metal. Different styles of air scoop were tried because this was considered to be the most vulnerable part of the aircraft. The first, 42-69647, had a much smaller, "clamshell" intake in the place of the regular intake. The second, 42-69769, had a flush intake. The third and fifth, 42-69769 and 42-69801, also had "clamshell" intakes, while the fourth, 42-69771, had a normal intake. The "clamshell" was adopted as standard. The RP-63A-11 had the same V-1710-93 of the A-9, but with water injection. Despite the significant weight increase, performance was very close to the standad P-63's. Because no external fuel tanks could be carried, the internal capacity was increased to 126 gal.

The production versions of the RP-63 were:

RP-63A-12—95 were produced, essentially identical to the first prototype.
RP-63C-2—The "Pinball" version of the P-63C. 1487.7 lb. of armor was carried. Serials: 43-10933—11132.
RP-63G-1—Two prototypes and 30 production examples were built. Basically a P-63 E with the V-1710-135 engine of 1200hp and 2164.9 lb. of armor. Serials: 43-11723—11724 and 45-57283—47312.

Zebra-striped P-39Qs were used as jump-ships, imitating enemy fighter tactics for the sake of bomber OTUs. They served as the predecessors of the RP-63 'Pinballs'. (Al Makiel)

Frangible Sal, the first RP-63A-11 is seen at the Yuma Army Airfield Flexible Gunnery School. Note the 'clamshell' intake. (Al Makiel)

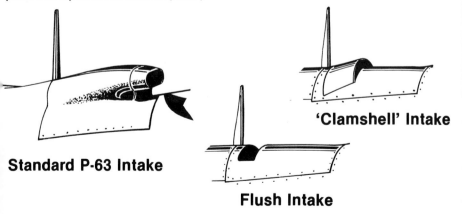

"Pinball", **subtitled** Do Not Tilt, **was an RP-63A with flush dorsal intake. A light in the propeller hub replaced the cannon. (USAF)**

Standard P-63 Intake

'Clamshell' Intake

Flush Intake

A pair of RP-63As. In the foreground is the initial prototype in its first form, with a flush intake. It tested that style before the 'clamshell' was adopted as standard. (USAF)

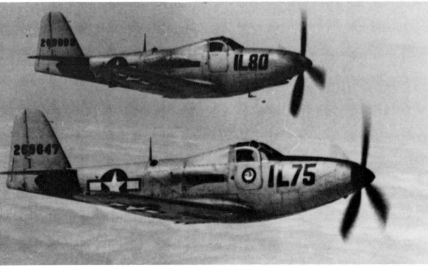

Two RP-63C-2s are seen on the ground. Because the C reverted to a normal air intake, only the greater thickness of the metal plate around the canopy and door show that these are 'armored'. Many RP-63Cs were used as target tugs rather than targets. (William Thompson and Balogh via Menard)

The RP-63G prototype (above) and two of the 30 production aircraft. These were totally dedicated to the job of target, with flush intake and lights inset into the fuselage to flash when the plane was hit. (Bell and Wm. Thompson)

L-39

As post war research into the realm of supersonic fight progressed, the swept wing seemed to hold the greatest promise. Since little was known about the behavior of such wings, a number of new test programs were initiated to gather additional data on the subject. One of these programs called for an investigation into the low speed behavior and the near sonic-speed characteristics of the wing. The Navy was given this area of research and in turn they asked Bell to provide a pair of swept wing aircraft which could be used to determine the low speed stability and stalling behavior, and to test Buseman's theories of the delta wing.

Bell engineers began with a pair of standard P-63C-5 Kingcobras. As the conversion work progressed problems developed with the center of gravity location. It was decided that this could be overcome by using a lighter propellor. At the time the Government was asking $1500.00 for a standard three bladed propellor but only $750.00 for a surplus P-39. Therefore, Bell bought a pair of P-39Q-10s from the War Assets Commission, obtaining the two propellors for the cost of one and getting a couple of Airacobras free. The new propellors replaced the four bladed ones and, after removing the old wings, the new 35 degree rearward swept wings were installed complete with slots and flaps. These aircraft were the first American airplanes of conventional design to have sweptback wings. They carried no armament and had the rear canopy blacked out. They were designated the L-39-1 and L-39-2.

The first flight was made with Bell test pilot A. M. 'Tex' Johnston at the controls and was relatively routine. As the test flights continued Chalmers H. 'Slick' Goodman, also a Bell test pilot, and Robert A. Champine, an ex-Navy fighter-bomber pilot working for NACA Langley, flew many of the data gathering flights.

As a result of some of the early flights the L-39-1 was modified by having the size of the leading edge slots reduced and a long ventral fin added under the aft fuselage. Data showed that the wing was inefficient at low speed. This led to the standard use of leading edge slats and greater wing areas to improve the low speed handling of swept wing fighters.

Despite the L-39 designation, its derivation from the P-63C-5, with its large ventral fin is obvious. The strings attached to the wings were filmed in flight by the pair of movie cameras mounted behind the canopy, to ascertain air flow over the wings. (Bell via E.J. Furler)

Part of the solution to the L-39's center of gravity problems was the fitting of the lighter, three-bladed prop from a P-39Q. (Al Makiel)

Bell modified one P-63 with a Vee-tail. The aircraft was lighter, cheaper to produce and had better handling. But the Air Force's attention by this time was taken up with jets, and this prototype was never repeated. (Bell)

The XFL-1 Airabonita was a navalized P-39 submitted for US Navy consideration in 1940, competing for the high speed, high altitude fighter specification issued in February 1938.

XFL-1 Airabonita

In 1938 one of the three new fighter projects initiated by the Navy was a carrier version of the Bell Airacobra which was ordered on 8 November 1938. Designated the XFL-1, a designation previously assigned to an abandoned Loening design of 1932, the new aircraft was to be called the Airabonita. Bell was using the prefix 'Aira' on its aircraft, by adding 'Bonita' they gave it a nautical flavor. The first flight of the XFL-1 took place on 13 May 1940. The aircraft was painted Navy grey overall except for the upper wing surfaces which were finished in chrome yellow. Bureau Number 1588 was assigned.

The Airabonita was actually quite different from the standard Airacobra. It featured a larger wing span with greater chord, a shorter fuselage and smaller rudder. The pilot's seat was higher which in turn meant that the canopy had to be higher. It was strengthened internally to stand the stress of carrier landings. The landing gear was changed to the conventional type since the Navy felt at that time that tricycle gear was not suited to carrier operations and an arresting gear and tail wheel were fitted. The gear was moved closer to the leading edge of the wing which in turn dictated a relocation of the wing root radiators. These were moved to exterior points under the rear of the central section of the wing. A small window was placed in the underside of the nose just forward of the wing roots to aid in carrier landings. The 1,150 hp liquid-cooled Allison XV-1710-6 was the first inline engine to be installed in a Naval fighter since 1928. Armament was to have been two .30 caliber machine guns firing through the cowling in the upper nose and one .50 caliber MG firing through the propellor hub.

Official evaluation by the Navy began in July 1940. Since the liquid-cooled engine ran contrary to the current Navy thinking the model was regarded with disfavor by many. Longitudinal stability was marginal and the vertical tail surfaces were enlarged after wind tunnel tests. Pilots objected to the small emergency hatch in the canopy preferring a jettisonable canopy. The vibration caused by the drive shaft was feared because it was felt that it might shorten the service life of the airplane. The expected service ceiling of 30,000 ft. was rarely attained. The project was eventually terminated because of these faults and because of the success of the F4U Corsair projects against which the XFL-1 was competing.

The Airabonita had a wing span of 35 ft. and was 29 ft. 9 1/8 in. long and stood 11 ft. 5 in. high. The wing area was 232 sq. ft. Normal weight was 6,651 lb., the maximum gross was 7,212 lb. and the empty weight stood at 5,161 lb. Fuel carried would vary from 162 to 200 gal. Top speed was 338 mph at 11,000 ft. and 307 mph at sea level. It cruised at 172 mph and landed at 72 mph. Best climb rate was 2,630 ft. per minute. Maximum range was 1,475 miles while normal range was 965 miles.

The Airabonita featured many differences from the XP-39, including the conventional landing gear, arrestor hook, smaller dorsal intake and wing root intakes moved underwing. The superior performance of the F4U Corsair, as well as structural problems with the FL-1 and the Navy's prejudice against inline engines, all conspired to doom the Airabonita. (US Navy via E. Furler)

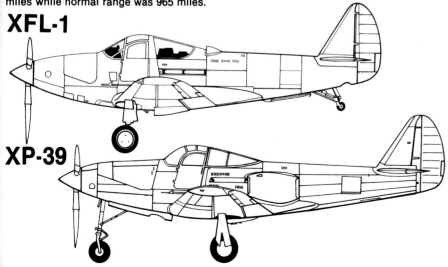

XFL-1

XP-39

Jack Woolams and Tex Johnston pose in front of the P-39Q racers which they flew with success in post-war air races, with semi-official factory support. Skylanes Unlimited was formed by a pair of ex-Bell employees. Both Cobra I & II were lightened by the removal of all military equipment, received uprated engines and four-bladed props. Cobra I, piloted by Woolams, was red and black. Cobra II was yellow and black. Cobra I and Woolams were lost over Lake Ontario after qualifying for the Cleveland Air Races in August 1946. Cobra II went on to win the 1946 Thompson Trophy with ease in Johnston's hands. It was raced again in 1947 and 1948, reaching 471mph that year. It crashed in 1969 while being used in an attempt to break the propeller-driven speed record. (Bell via Earl Reinert)